Logotherapy Surviving Holocaust: Viktor Frankl

Logotherapy Surviving Holocaust: Viktor Frankl

Written & Edited By:

Dr. Austin Mardon
Dr. Catherine Mardon
Naima Mohamood
Sriraam Sivachandran
Paige Breedon
Sameen Ali
Alexa Gee
Hafsa Alamagan
Amal Mohammed
Hafsah Clare

Cover Design By:

Aleia Cabote

Copyright © 2021 by Austin Mardon

All rights reserved. This book or any portion thereof may not be reproduced or used in any manner whatsoever without the express written permission of the publisher except for the use of brief quotations in a book review or scholarly journal.

First Printing: 2021

Typeset and Cover Design by Aleia Cabote

ISBN 978-1-77369-432-0

Golden Meteorite Press
103 11919 82 St NW
Edmonton, AB T5B 2W3
www.goldenmeteoritepress.com

Table of Contents

Chapter 1:
The Philosophies of Logotherapy Surviving Holocaust: Viktor Frankl 07

Chapter 2:
Impacts of Logotherapy to Society 15

Chapter 3:
What is Logotherapy Surviving Holocaust: Viktor Frankl 23

Chapter 4:
Holocaust Viktor Frankl and the Link to Science 33

References 43

Chapter 1
The Philosophies of Logotherapy Surviving Holocaust: Viktor Frankl
by Sriraam Sivachandran

Introduction

Throughout the history of the world, there have been several moments where the humanity of some had been taken away due to the unfortunate superiority some groups of people had over others. In the present world, people are faced with situations that make them extremely uncomfortable or anxious and they do not know how to deal and cope with these situations by themselves. Therefore, they utilise experts such as therapists that may know certain exercises or methods that would ease their state of mind. This concept is no different if it had to be applied to people that suffered through the more famous crisis in history. There have been numerous situations that have occurred in history in which people would have needed a proper method of therapy in order to cope with the distress that they endured. However, some of the techniques and methods that therapists use today may not have been practiced at those specific periods of time, thus leaving those people to deal with their horrid situation by themselves. However, on the off chance, there are situations where survivors of mass casualties deliver important therapeutic ideas and methods based on their life and their experiences during their distress. An example of this can be observed when talking about the Holocaust.

The Holocaust

The Holocaust is one of the most polarizing and unfortunate mass causalities that took place against a single group people in the history of the world. The Nazis and their allies were responsible for the murders of an estimated six million Jewish civilians and other racial groups that were deemed inferior (United States Holocaust Memorial Museum, 2021). Nazis and their allies would kill races deemed inferior when they would go on raids to various villages in countries such as Poland and the Soviet Union (United States Holocaust Memorial Museum, 2021). However, they would also force millions of people to work under severe conditions, such as starvation and neglect, which would ultimately lead numerous more deaths (United States Holocaust Memorial Museum, 2021). However, after the end of the Nazi regime and the end of the Holocaust, there were some survivors that were finally free of the devasting tyranny. Nonetheless, after suffering physically, mentally, and psychologically for so long, these survivors had a hard time with living with what they saw and what they specifically endured for such a long time. Certain therapeutic methods and interventions that can be categorized as conventional did not ameliorate the psychological state due to the fact that the trauma they suffered was exponentially greater compared to the psychological stresses of someone suffering from everyday situations. The survivors of the Holocaust had to be treated with psychological therapy that was founded just for them and the only way for this to happen would be for the founder to understand what actually occurred to these numerous survivors during their Holocaust experience. This came into fruition when Dr. Viktor Emil Frankl, a Holocaust survivor himself, created an unconventional method of psychological therapy, called logotherapy, that would help the survivors of the Holocaust deal with their past traumatic experiences.

Dr. Viktor Frankl's Journey

Before diving into the work of Dr. Frankl and his great research on the psychological therapy of logotherapy, it is important to understand his journey and the overall perception of him that has stood in place since his work truly had a great impact on the psychological therapeutic community. Throughout his life, Dr. Frankl continuously published several papers that had a focus on individual psychology and social reform (Viktor Frankl Institute, 1992). His overall goal was to understand the relationship between psychotherapy and philosophy which would in turn provide a clearer image of the certain values (Viktor Frankl Institute, 1992). Twhe first time that Dr. Frankl started to broach the idea of logotherapy was in 1926 because he wanted to understand what it actually meant to undergo mental healing (Viktor Frankl Institute, 1992). Throughout his life, Dr. Frankl was known for his constant work to help with the youth of Vienna. For example, with the help of other psychologists he offered free psychological counselling to adolescents (Viktor Frankl Institute, 1992). He also held a counseling initiative at the end of the school term that would result in a great decrease in the overall student suicide rate (Viktor Frankl Institute, 1992). In the year of 1937, Dr. Frankl was finally able to open a private practice for neurology and psychiatry, but it was later closed down due to the severe restrictions put in place against Jewish doctors (Viktor Frankl Institute, 1992). However, in 1940 he was able to become the director of the neurological department of a clinic that aided Jewish patients (Viktor Frankl Institute, 1992). During his time as the department head, Dr. Frankl saved numerous mentally ill patients from being euthanized by the Nazis by providing false diagnoses (Viktor Frankl Institute, 1992). Unfortunately, in the year 1942, Dr. Frankl, his wife, and his parents were all sent to the Terezin Ghetto, a concentration camp located in the Czech Republic (Viktor Frankl Institute, 1992). Even in the concentration camp, he tried to help the inmates that were suffering from psychological crises and those who were contemplating suicide (Viktor Frankl Institute, 1992). Unfortunately, he was separated from his wife and mother, since he was transferred to concentration camps focussed on labour while his wife and mother were sent to another camp (Viktor Frankl Institute, 1992). After the liberation of his concentration camp in 1945, he went to Vienna, Austria to find out what happened to his family members and sadly he learned about the death of his wife, mother, and brother (Viktor Frankl Institute, 1992). In order to cope with his trauma, he started to write several books that would be focused on his thoughts on resilience and the importance of embracing life in the face of adversity (Viktor Frankl Institute, 1992).

Based on this information that is available on Dr. Frankl, it is quite obvious what his life's journey was about. Dr. Frankl's purpose in life was to help as many people as he could, and this could be seen throughout his whole life. He helped children and adolescents that were suffering from psychological problems and that had a great impact in decreasing the total number of suicides. He did not have to do this, but it was in his nature to help people have a clear psychological slate with no distresses. As soon as he became a licensed medical doctor, he helped a large number of patients a year, and this occurred during the time when the Nazis were oppressing Jewish doctors. Finally, even after being captured by the Nazis and being placed in concentration camps, he tired to ease the psychological fears of his fellow inmates who were contemplating suicide. His overall journey can be remembered as a man facing adversity that avoided every obstacle to help those in need.

Logotherapy

While Dr. Frankl was famous for various books and papers that he published, one of the more famous concepts that he founded was logotherapy. Some survivors of the Holocaust do not respond to the conventional psychological treatment methods due to the fact that they are not conditioned to help people that suffered trauma as great as the Holocaust. However, logotherapy was created by Dr. Frankl to help those survivors that needed a novel treatment method to deal with the psychological trauma of the Holocaust. The goal of logotherapy is to break through the dimensions of an individual's life that allows them to forego the boundaries and constraints that have been set in their life (Kimble & Ellor, 2021). An individual utilising logotherapy will try to ignite their will to meaning (Kimble & Ellor, 2021). Logotherapy allows the patient to see that they can elicit a response through their own freedom regardless of their desires and their situation (Kimble & Ellor, 2021). It gives the patient a chance to see that they have several options when it comes to decisions and desires of their everyday lives (Kimble & Ellor, 2021). Logotherapy gives the patients an opportunity to see that there are even options to certain decisions and desires during extremely oppressive situations and the mere change of their mentality or attitude can ignite a different and positive response to the specific situation (Kimble & Ellor, 2021). In terms of the Holocaust survivors, logotherapy would allow those survivors a chance to give their own unique response to certain decisions and desires they may have after suffering through their trauma and they may not have this ability with another psychological treatment option. One of the main reasons as to why logotherapy is an important tool to treat people that suffered from a great trauma is that it was founded by someone who themselves suffered from a great trauma. Dr. Frankl explained that it is hard for outsiders to understand what went on inside the camp and how little value was placed on their lives (Piccirillo, 2021).

While the understanding and further development of the concept of logotherapy occurred later in Dr. Frankl's life, the initial idea of logotherapy came into fruition before and during his time in the concentration camps in the Czech Republic. Like all the other Holocaust sufferers, he witnessed one of the greatest examples of human suffering through his own experiences and his own eyes. Since he had a psychological background, he was able to analyze the psychological state of his fellow prisoners and himself as well (Piccirillo, 2021). Another aspect that is important toward the concept of logotherapy is that it forces the patient to look ahead to their future beyond their current situation (Piccirillo, 2021). What is the patient's meaning of life? What is their primary motivation in life? When linking this back to the Holocaust, it can be said that some survivors may have a strong moral character (Piccirillo, 2021). However, it is important to note that Dr. Frankl also states that survival also has a huge varying factor of luck that could lead to the prolonged survival or ultimate death (Piccirillo, 2021). Nonetheless, he explained that if someone is able to suffer bravely till their last moment, their life has a meaning until their literal end (Piccirillo, 2021). The meaning of life of a prisoner in the concentration camp is different compared to the meaning of life of a free person. While the meaning of life varies based on the situation, specific meanings of life can be associated with the specific situation (Piccirillo, 2021). For example, the meaning of life for the prisoners of the concentration camps can actually be found in suffering (Piccirillo, 2021). At the core of every person, based on logotherapy, people are constantly aiming to find the meaning of life (Piccirillo, 2021). Even through the constant suffering of the extreme trauma in the concentration camps, some prisoners are able to see their meaning of life and with a factor of luck, certain people were able to survive.

Conclusion

It is always important to understand the history that surrounds various groups of people and how they overcame their specific trauma. The Holocaust is widely known as one of the most traumatic mass genocides that occurred in human history. However, something that does not get talked about enough is the survivors and their mental states. Conventional psychological treatment methods were and still are not enough to help those that have suffered an extreme traumatic event. Dr. Frankl, a Holocaust survivor, experienced and witnessed firsthand the trauma that prisoners in concentration camps had to go through on a daily basis. Using his experience, he was able to build upon his theory of logotherapy that allows patients to look into their future and discover their meaning of life. Even though there was such a great number of deaths in the concentration camps, the fact that there were survivors supports the concept of logotherapy. Many survivors were able to see their meaning of life through their suffering and had a strong moral character that allowed them to overcome the trauma they faced on a daily basis.

Chapter 2
Impacts of Logotherapy to Society
by Paige Breedon

Introduction

Logotherapy is a form of psychotherapy that focuses on the future and an individual's ability to endure hardships and suffering through a search for purpose (Cuncic, 2021). Dr. Viktor Frankl, a well-known psychiatrist and psychotherapist, developed logotherapy after becoming a Holocaust survivor, and thus this theory is reflective of his experiences of immense trauma and suffering (Cuncic, 2021). Logotherapy's basis is grounded in his book, published in 1946: "Man's Search for Meaning," which provides a recount of his experiences in a Nazi-run concentration camp and his consequential theories that lead to the emergence of logotherapy (Cuncic, 2021). Throughout this chapter, emphasis will be put on how Viktor Frankl's logotherapy and consistent experiences have impacted society. Specifically, the impact of logotherapy can be viewed from different perspectives relative to the human experience, academia, and medicine and continues to be relevant today when analyzing human behaviour and thought patterns. Overall, Viktor Frankl can be considered a pioneer experiencing immense suffering and managing to survive, and his insights have helped to guide many survivors and professionals in overcoming hardships and moving forward with a more positive and purposeful outlook.

Impact on the Human Experience

Unambiguously, the Holocaust marked a period of immense suffering and was ultimately a vile manifestation of human evil. The aftermath of the Holocaust was uncharted territory to a 20th-century society in the way that it marked the beginning of a new type of people: 'survivors' (Piccirillo, 2010). Survivors' can be defined as people who have endured extreme hardship and suffering (Piccirillo, 2010). These 'survivors' had to figure out ways to cope with their past traumatic experiences while simultaneously re-entering society (Piccirillo, 2010). Following the Holocaust, conventional psychotherapy was insufficient in helping treat and re-integrate survivors, and therefore new theories and outlooks on suffering and surviving were needed. Also, following the Holocaust, a significant difference in knowledge and experience drove a significant divide between people who had experienced concentration camps and those unscathed from that burden. As Frankl put it, "We dislike talking about our experiences. No explanation is needed for those who have been inside, and the others will understand neither how we felt then nor how we feel now" (Piccirillo, 2010; Frankl, 1946, p. 24). Frankl's statement clearly illustrates the way a traumatic experience like attending a concentration camp can make those who survive feel outcast from society. These are some of the challenges that the aftermath of the Holocaust brought, and they required new insight to understand and overcome said challenges. That is where the work of Dr. Viktor Frankl became especially relevant as he had experienced the traumatic effects of the Holocaust himself and had experienced life before and after his time in a concentration camp that helped him to understand better the differences between operating in society and operating in the space of suffering and hardship. Also, "Man's Search for Meaning" became a helpful resource in examining the experience of a concentration camp survivor and perhaps providing better insight for the members of society fortunate enough not to have lived this reality. Frankl's book outlines the basis of logotherapy, the school of psychiatric thought he created based on his theories surrounding suffering and human existence established pre-Holocaust and tested through his own experiences.

Moreover, Frankl's ideas and logotherapy in general have helped humans better understand the complicated situation that followed the Holocaust and continues to help people in the field of psychotherapy ("Logotherapy", 2015). It is also important to acknowledge that specific lessons relative to the human experience have been quite impactful since right after the Holocaust till today and are embodied in the form of the techniques of logotherapy. Specifically, logotherapy techniques that are ultimately reflective of critical lessons and the teachings of Viktor Frankl include dereflection, paradoxical intention, and Socratic dialogue ("Logotherapy", 2015). These techniques are all part of modern logotherapy intervention, and at the root of them lies a key lesson that can help one better understand the human experience and its search for meaning. Firstly, dereflection is a technique of logotherapy that redirects one's attention from themselves onto something else to combat the issue of self-absorption ("Logotherapy", 2015). Secondly, paradoxical intention entails a person asking for the thing they fear the most. This technique uses humour and ridicule to treat people facing anxiety and phobias and ultimately helps to reduce fear and various anxious symptoms ("Logotherapy", 2015). Lastly, Socratic dialogue is also a common hallmark of logotherapy and entails a logotherapist using a patient's words as a method of self-discovery; this technique allows a person to see new meaning in the way they speak and think ("Logotherapy", 2015). These techniques embody a different virtue value to Frankl's logotherapy and reflect his experience and expertise as a psychotherapist.

Additionally, to summarize the most quintessential aspects of Frankl's experience and teaching would require acknowledging what Frankl considers how to find meaning ("Logotherapy", 2015). Specifically, Frankl suggests that one can discover meaning in three different ways: by creating a work or accomplishing a task, by experiencing something fully or loving someone, and by one's attitude toward suffering ("Logotherapy", 2015). Perhaps, the last method Frankl proposes strikes home with himself as he has said: "the last of human freedoms - the ability to choose one's attitude in a given set of circumstances" as well "a human being is a deciding being" ("Logotherapy", 2015; Viktor E., n.d.). These quotations, along with his known experience in concentration camps, show that despite being in unimaginable suffering and hardship, he still looks forward optimistically and intends to choose his attitude and reaction to external problems and chaos. The idea of freedom of will is also a pillar in logotherapy as Frankl attributes freedom of will as the essence of human existence (Wong, 2017).

Moreover, in Frankl's book "Man's Search for Meaning," he outlines the steps associated with adjusting to life in a concentration camp ("Viktor," 2011). Hopefully, the need to adjust to such an evil and horrific environment and situation will never be required again. The steps can still be relevant for one who wants to better adjust to a period of immense suffering. These stages include shock or denial, apathy towards others, and depersonalization, bitterness, moral distortion, and disillusionment for survivors ("Viktor," 2011). All of these stages were experienced by

Frankl, when he attended a concentration camp, and perhaps others experiencing hardships can use this wisdom in their own way.

Impact on Academia

Dr. Viktor Frankl's logotherapy has made an impact on the field of psychology and psychotherapy. Before Frankl's time in a concentration camp, he was a psychologist and psychotherapist, and while he was working in these positions, he came up with theories and perspectives on the meaning of life and suffering. It was not until he endured the Holocaust that these theories were tested and proved to the extent that he entered them into the realm of academia ("Viktor," 2011). Considering Frankl's academic and real-life experience makes his ideas and contributions to psychotherapy and the meaning of life that much more credible and relevant. Before Frankl's time, other great psychotherapists and psychology experts had their own ideas on meaning and life. Most notably, logotherapy is an extension of philosopher Soren Kierkegaard's 'will to meaning' ("Viktor," 2011). Both Frankl and Kierkegaard's ideas contradict Sigmund Freud as he believes that people are driven towards pleasure and sex rather than discovering their true purpose ("Viktor," 2011). It also contradicts the ideas of Nietzsche and Alder as they both believed that humans live for power rather than meaning ("Viktor," 2011). Overall, Frankl has brought a unique perspective to the academic table and helped further develop a new school of thought relevant to psychotherapy which has an immensely notable impact.

Impact on Medicine/Clinical Practice

As logotherapy has gained traction, some practicing physicians, psychotherapists, and related professionals have started to integrate the techniques and teachings of logotherapy in a clinical setting. For instance, a study identifying the effectiveness of group logotherapy on Iran university students serves as an example of how logotherapy can help to reduce depression and increase feelings of meaningfulness (Robatmili et al., 2015). This study involved ten students in the experimental group and ten students in the control group (Robatmili et al., 2015). Instruments like the Purpose in Life (PIL) test and Beck Depression Inventory (BDI) were used to assess students' feelings of meaningfulness and depression, respectively (Robatmili et al., 2015). The experimental group participated in 10 logotherapy sessions, while the control group abstained from logotherapy (Robatmili et al., 2015). The mean scores for depression levels were lower and meaning in life higher in the experimental group than the control (Robatmili et al., 2015). These results ultimately suggest logotherapy as a viable form of treatment for patients suffering from depression or individuals who want to find meaning in life (Robatmili et al., 2015). Although this study could improve by increasing the number of test subjects, it still warrants further investigation and optimism for the benefit of logotherapy. Overall, logotherapy has significantly evolved from the ideas of Viktor Frankl to an experimentally tested theory to be applicable in the clinic or a practical environment. All of these stages that logotherapy has undergone have impacted society, and as this field continues to develop, society should be prepared to reap more benefits from the knowledge and experiences of Viktor Frankl.

Another study proposed that logotherapy could help improve mental health among said demographic, thus providing strong optimism to support logotherapy as a despicable psychotherapy treatment (Rahgozar & Giménez-Llort, 2020). A common issue faced by immigrants and those seeking asylum is a greater vulnerability to mental health-related problems such as depression, anxiety, and posttraumatic stress disorder (PTSD) (Rahgozar & Giménez-Llort, 2020). The study attempted to investigate whether logotherapy would be a helpful form of psychotherapy to ease the mental health burden on immigrants in the third millennium and assist them in finding meaning in life (Rahgozar & Giménez-Llort, 2020). The review also acknowledged that it could be specifically advantageous for helping immigrants with diverse backgrounds because logotherapy was developed from a multicultural perspective (Rahgozar & Giménez-Llort, 2020). The paper concluded that considering immigrants and their unique challenges; logotherapy seems to be an appropriate means of treatment that could increase mental health among a diverse population (Rahgozar & Giménez-Llort, 2020). Hopefully, these kinds of proposals will continue to transition to action and intervention and to consider logotherapy's diverse potential; logotherapy should also continue to impact large groups of people well into the future positively.

Furthermore, another review paper also suggested that logotherapy could be helpful for the workforce, specifically for those experiencing feelings of being burnt out (Riethof & Bob, 2019). The study discussed how research has shown that logotherapy and other disciplines and ideas related to existential meaning and life fulfillment could help to understand better, prevent, and combat burnout syndrome (Riethof & Bob, 2019). Burnout syndrome is defined as a state of total exhaustion often due to work exhaustion or work stress (Riethof & Bob, 2019). Ultimately, the review warrants further investigation into how burnout syndrome could be resolved by using the teachings of logotherapy to ground one in a journey to discover themselves. Overall, this study opens up another demographic of people who could benefit from Dr. Frankl's expertise in psychotherapy and experiences dealing with suffering while simultaneously seeking self-fulfillment.

Viktor Frankl and logotherapy have immensely helped in academia, and clinically, many experiments and reviews have proved and proposed logotherapy as a viable option to increase one's mental health and overall sense of self. Although this chapter only discussed examples of students, immigrants, and employees facing feelings of anxiety and distress, everyone could benefit from seeking to discover their self-fulfillment journey. That is why logotherapy is so fundamental to psychotherapy, and some consider it to be its own school of thought within the discipline.

Conclusion

In conclusion, Viktor Frankl is a well-known individual for his immense contributions. Such include helping the world better understand the human experience, creating a school of thought relevant to psychotherapy, and providing a viable form of treatment (logotherapy) that can be used in clinical settings and help implement real change in a person's attitude and mental health. Through his own academic and personal journey, Frankl has learned and taught many relevant lessons that help one better understand and tolerate great suffering while simultaneously finding a greater sense of meaning. He has also developed logotherapy which has many great techniques to help people overcome their selfishness, fears and better understand their thinking patterns. Not all in the field of psychotherapy agree or have previously agreed with Frankl's answer to what is the root of human existence, but he has undoubtedly opened the floor for conversation and created a theory backed by his own real-life experiences. The ideas and trauma of Viktor Frankl today can be seen being instituted in psychotherapy clinics promoting real change. Overall, the impact of Viktor Frankl and logotherapy is significant for large populations, the field of psychotherapy, and practicing therapists and related professionals.

Chapter 3
What is Logotherapy Surviving Holocaust: Viktor Frankl
by Sameen Ali

Introduction

Trauma is an unfortunate fact of life. Oftentimes, life is uncontrollable leaving damaging long-term disasters lingering behind. However, trauma does not have to be a life sentence. There are various coping methods and different forms of therapy that can be sought out in hopes to surpass the horrors that took place. Although trauma comes in all shapes and forms – the horrific event that created a group of individuals that experienced what no one could even fathom was the Holocaust. Holocaust survivors were forced to cope with the first-hand encounter of the capacity of human evil (Piccirillo, 2010). These survivors did not only struggle to live during the agonizing years the atrocious event took place but even after liberation (Piccirillo, 2010). Although their bodies may have been liberated – the damage, shock and horrors experienced were long term. These individuals stood out from the rest of the worlds 'normal' and anyone who did not have to live through the camps could not even begin to imagine the pains that they endured. Hence, conventional psychological therapy would not even begin to wash away the emotional damage of the holocaust survivors (Piccirillo, 2010).

Survivors are pioneers of human coping. They were forced to live in a world that divided their psychological nature to extremes – any attempts on understanding their pain was to no avail considering the severity of that they endured. When others attempted to ask about their experience, this psychological divide became more apparent. A very common reply to questions asked about their trauma was, "we dislike talking about our experiences. No explanations are needed for those who have been inside, and the others will understand neither how we felt then nor how we feel now," (Piccirillo, 2010). Dr Viktor E Frankl, a holocaust survivor and psychiatrist – both before and after his concentration camp experience – developed existential psychotherapy known as logotherapy in which he attempts to bridge the gap and unite all men in their struggles to find meaning in life (Piccirillo, 2010). This chapter will not only discuss what logotherapy is but how it was effective and the outcomes. In addition, it will explore how Dr Frankl created this therapy and where his ideas stemmed from.

Who is Viktor Frankl?

Viktor Frankl was a 20th century psychiatrist, he was a holocaust survivor and wrote a best selling book – Man's Search for Meaning. Victor Emil Frankl was born on March 26, 1905 in Vienna, Austria (GoodTherapy Team, 2019). Frankle received his MD and PhD degree from the University of Vienna where he studied psychiatry and neurology, focusing on suicide and depression (GoodTherapy Team, 2019). As a medical student, he reached out to highschool students struggling with depression to help eliminate suicide (GoodTherapy Team, 2019). His accomplishments lead to him heading the suicide prevention department of the General Hospital in Vienna. Frankle treated thousands of people over the four years and took a position as the head of the neurological department at the Rothschild Hospital. This was one of the few facilities that allowed Jews to practice medicine at that time (GoodTherapy Team, 2019).

In 1942, Frankl and his parents, wife, and brother were arrested and sent to the Theresienstadt concentration camp. Unfortunately, his father only survived for six months (GoodTherapy Team, 2019). Although Frankl lived, he was moved between four concentration camps, including Auschwitz where both his mother and brother died (GoodTherapy Team, 2019). Frankl's wife died at Bergen-Belson (GoodTherapy Team, 2019). In 1945 Frankl's concentration camp was liberated – after the liberation Frankl learned that all his immediate family members had died, except his sister who had emigrated to Australia (GoodTherapy Team, 2019). In the camps, Frankl and fellow prisoners made an effort to address the psychological impact on other inmates (GoodTherapy Team, 2019). In an effort to prevent suicicde attempts Frankl and others aided other inmates who faced severe depression by encouraging them to reflect on positive memories and thoughts they had (GoodTherapy Team, 2019).

This experience in the camps to develop his theory of logotherapy, which is also referred to as "Third Viennese School of Psychotherapy," this name originated since Frankl came after Sigmund Freud and Alfred Adler (GoodTherapy Team, 2019). Frankl believed that even in the midst of such dehumanizing and atrocious conditions, life still had meaning and that suffering had a purpose (GoodTherapy Team, 2019). Frankl thought that during that in extreme conditions, an individual could escape though their spiritual self in order to survive circumstances that seem unbearable (GoodTherapy Team, 2019). Frankl believed that the spiritual self could not be impacted by the circumstances around an individual or any external forces (GoodTherapy Team, 2019). Frankl spent a lot of time studying existential methods of therapy which is a style of therapy that places emphasis on the human condition as a whole. This style of therapy uses a positive approach that applauds human capacities and aspirations while simultaneously acknowledging human limitations (GoodTherapy Team, 2019). Existential psychotherapy has many similarities with humanistic psychology, experiential psychotherapy, depth psychotherapy, and relational psychotherapy (GoodTherapy Team, 2019).

In his book Man's Search for Meaning, Frankl writes the detailed perspective of living through the horrors of the concentration camps. Frankl was a professor of neurology and psychiatry at the University of Vienna from 1948-1990, and he directed the neurology department at the Vienna Polyclinic Hospital between 1946 and 1970 (GoodTherapy Team, 2019). Frankl was incredibly successful throughout his career. Not only did he publish numerous books but he also received dozens of honorary degrees, lectured around the world and served as a guest professor in universities such as Harvard (GoodTherapy Team, 2019). In addition, his contribution to psychology was significant (GoodTherapy Team, 2019). His book has been widely cited as one of the most important and inspirational books of the 20th century (GoodTherapy Team, 2019). His book outlines three phases of adapting to life in a concentration camp. These phases include:

1. Shock or denial during initial admission
2. Apathy toward others
3. Depersonalization, bitterness and disillusionment for survivors

Frankl argues that finding meaning in everyday moments can enable trauma survivors to avoid the bitterness and apathy that are so often the result of the torture and trauma that was endured (GoodTherapy Team, 2019). Frankl encouraged sufferers to think of people they would noy want to disappoint, such as dead family members and reflect on how they would be viewed by them (GoodTherapy Team, 2019). Frankl believed meaning can be found through creativity and work, human interactions and experience. Frankl's logotherapy is based on the philosopher Soren Kierkegaard's "will to meaning." Frankl draws upon Soren Kierkegaard's philosophy in arguing that the primary drive in life is the search for meaning. Not any form of pleasure, as Freud would theorize (GoodTherapy Team, 2019). Logotherapy is a form of existential therapy that focuses on the fact that people have the power to find meaning in anything they do (GoodTherapy Team, 2019).

What is logotherapy surviving the holocaust?

Frankl believed that "he who has a reason to live can bear with almost any how." In other words, the human struggle is the search for meaning in life, a reason to live and he believed that all other actions and experiences were secondary to that (Piccirillo, 2010). Frankle explained how, "Logotherapy focuses on the meaning of human existence as well as on the man's search for such a meaning." He outlines the beliefs of logotherapy through a subjective narrative of his Holocaust experiences (Piccirillo, 2010).

During the Holocaust, Frankl witnessed extremes of human suffering (Piccirillo, 2010). He watched fear destroy men, and watch sufferers find ways to hold onto hope and humanity. His psychological background compelled him to psychoanalyze prisoners and himself (Piccirillo, 2010). Frankle believed that abnormal reactions to an abnormal situation is normal. He also attempted to explain what it was like for the sufferers to others. However, Frankl explained that, "it is very difficult for an outsider to grasp how little value was placed on human life in these camps," (Piccirillo, 2010).

In his book, Frankl uses anecdotal evidence to help readers empathise with the situation. Dr. Frankl's more controversial claim is that survival is linked to free will (Piccirillo, 2010). These controversies are later discussed in chapter 10. However, Frankl attempted to back this claim up, "the experiences of camp life show that man does have a choice of action (Piccirillo, 2010). There were enough examples, often of a heroic nature, which proved that apathy could be overcome, irritability suppressed (Piccirillo, 2010). Man can preserve a vestige of spiritual freedom, of independence of mind, even in such terrible conditions of psychic and physical stress." Frankl also explained how the camps "tore open the human soul and exposed its depths," (Piccirillo, 2010).

Logotherapy is based on theories that were formed by Dr Frankl earlier in his life but were affirmed after his experience in the Holocause (Piccirillo, 2010). It is a different approach compared to psychoanalysis. Logotherapy asks its patients to look towards their future circumstances (Piccirillo, 2010). Frankl explained how, "In logotherapy the patient is actually confronted and reoriented with the meaning of his life," (Piccirillo, 2010). The central principle of logotherapy is what Dr Frankl calls "the will to meaning," accordingly, "man's search for meaning gia primarily the motive in his life and not a secondary realization of instinctual drive," (Piccirillo, 2010).

The patient is helped not only by analyzing facts about his/her psych but also by aiding them ingraspign their own meaning of life (Piccirillo, 2010). One of the most important aspects of logotherapy is its subjective adaptability; it doesn't seek to provide universal truths for all humans; however, Dr Frankl explained how it does "the specific meaning of a person's life at a given moment," (Piccirillo, 2010). Dr Frankl believed that the patient is responsible for his/her own decisions, conclusion and conscience. They're also responsible for discovering their own life's meaning (Piccirillo, 2010).

Dr Frankle believed that the only way to grasp another human being in the innermost core of their personality is through love (Piccirillo, 2010). In this context, love does not imply sexual or romantic connotation, instead it is used to fully understand another human being by realizing the potential within the person. This would allow the person to "actualize these potentialities," (Piccirillo, 2010). Frankl also explained how "the meaning of suffering" is the most important aspect of logotherapy when considering the Holocaust (Piccirillo, 2010). It is a clear demonstration of the method that helped him survive the concentration camp. Dr Frankle explains how the human ability to channel suffering into potential for achievement (Piccirillo, 2010).

In his own words, Frankl encompasses what it means to have survived the Holocaust:

"We must never forget that we may also find meaning in life even when confronted with a hopeless situation. When facing a fate that cannot be changed. For what then matters is to bear witness to the uniquely human potential at its best, which is to transform a personal tragedy into a triumph, to turn one's predicament into a human achievement, " (Piccirillo, 2010).

Effectiveness of logotherapy

It is vital to proceed with cation when applying psychological thoeries to the Holocaust (Piccirillo, 2010). This is because of the incredible abnormality of the situation. Holocaust survivor and Nobel Prize laureate Elie Eirsel mistakenly claimed that "no theory hold when it comes to the holocause," (Piccirillo, 2010). Logotherapy is uniquely and not easily let go of (Piccirillo, 2010). The fact that it was founded by a Holocuast survivor whose tragic experiences confirmed his beliefs gives the theory credibility (Piccirillo, 2010).

Frankl's aim was to assess how life in the concentration camp reflected in the mind of the average prisoner and this assessment confirmed the theories he stated (Piccirillo, 2010). It is from his first hand experience along with his fellow prisoners that he came to the conclusions that he did. Even when he was stripped to his very core, his primal purpose is a search for the meaning of life (Piccirillo, 2010). To dismiss the validity of logotherapy simply because it is a "theory: is a mistake, as Dr. Frankl is not a third party observer but rather a first hand witness of the cruelties that took place (Piccirillo, 2010).

The fact that people of strong moral character and unbreakable will perished in the atrocities is a possible counterexample; however, Dr. Frankl never claimed that the will to survive necessarily led to survival, instead he claims that, "the sort of person the prisoner beame was the result of an inner decision" This inner decision is related to survival as the person isn't murdered or otherwise physically inhibited (Piccirillo, 2010). Frankl understood that luck played a crucial role when it came to determining who survived (Piccirillo, 2010).

Many may reject Fankl's theory being applied to the Holocaust because most are developed to explain the "normal" world (Piccirillo, 2010). However, the fact that this principle can apply anywhere does not diminish logotherapy's credibility (Piccirillo, 2010). Dr. Frankl admits that though each life has meaning, that meaning is relative to each person (Piccirillo, 2010). He understood that the meaning of the life of a condemned concentration camp inmate differs from a free individual. The inmate has limited resources, unlike the average individual. Dr. Frankl said, "everyone's task is as unique as his specific opportunity to implement it". He later asserts that life's meaning can even be discovered in suffering (Piccirillo, 2010). De Frankl built a credible thoery by examining core of human nature he witnessed in Holocaust (Piccirillo, 2010). Unlike the traditional psychoanalysis methods, he did not rely on outside experience to explain what he witnessed (Piccirillo, 2010).

Conclusion

Logotherapy was established in order to help holocuast survivors cope. However, it can be applied to anyone. The meaning of life is essential to keep moving forward. Dr Frankl's struggles and personal experience along with studying his inmates helped him develop this theory. These facts establish credibility in logotherapy. Dr. Frankl emphasises the fact that even when suffering one must find a meaning in life. He supports individuals reaching into their spiritual side to aid in times of suffering. Frankl was a strong believer that the spiritual side cannot be impacted by external factors. Trauma is indeed an unfortunate fact of life, however – even trauma as incomprehensible as the concentration camps can be coped with. Dr. Frankl is proof that indeed, trauma does not have to be a life sentence.

Chapter 4
Holocaust Viktor Frankl and the Link to Science:
by Alexa Gee

Introduction

The Holocaust was a traumatic and deeply scarring event for millions of people. The few who survived suffered from painful memories for the rest of their lives (Piccirillo, 2010). Psychologists who studied the Holocaust survivors observed the immense struggle to heal from the pain that had been inflicted upon them. In the mid-1900s, therapy was unable to fully rehabilitate many from their trauma, given the extreme nature of what they had gone through.

Dr. Viktor E. Frankl, a Jewish psychiatrist survived the Holocaust (Piccirillo, 2010). In his book, Man's Search for Meaning, he discusses his experiences and his observations on the psychology of the other prisoners in the concentration camps. He saw that some inmates held onto hope even in dire circumstances. In his book, he said that "Man can preserve a vestige of spiritual freedom, of independence of mind, even in such terrible conditions of psychic and physical stress" (Frankl, 1992, p. 86). His somewhat controversial claim is that survival is linked to free will (Piccirillo, 2010). This came from seeing some prisoners retaining mental autonomy even while physically restrained. Through watching his fellow prisoners, Dr. Frankl developed the concept of logotherapy.

In this chapter, the science behind logotherapy will be discussed as well as how it has been used in the 21st century to treat and help patients cope with various mental and physiological disorders.

Psychology of Logotherapy

Logotherapy is a method different from first and second-wave psychology (Cohut, 2018). The first wave involves psychoanalysis developed by Freud. Traditional psychoanalysis relies on introspection and retrospection to treat the mind (Piccirillo, 2010). The second school of psychotherapy involves Alfred Adler's concept of inferiority feeling (Cohut, 2018). Instead, as the third school of psychotherapy, logotherapy asks patients to look forward to their future circumstances (Cohut, 2018; Piccirillo, 2010) Logotherapy was originally called height psychology to explain it in opposition to Freud's concept of depth psychology to psychoanalyze the unconscious mind (Devoe, 2012). Height psychology asks the person to go beyond this by seeking to find their purpose in life, no matter what stage and in all types of circumstances.

Logotherapy can be considered a type of existential psychology (Devoe, 2012). This type of psychology postulates that therapists must immerse themselves in the existence of the patient so they can understand them fully (Spear, n.d.). The patients learn to understand the life they are living, by reflecting on the purpose, values, and position in life.

Frankl states that "man's search for meaning is the primary motivation in his life and not a secondary rationalization of instinctual drives" (Frankl, 1992, p.121). In other words, logotherapy asks patients to ponder the meaning of life, which is responsible for a person's conscience, decisions, and conclusions. The answer to the meaning of life is not universal; it is specific and unique for each person, shaped by experiences (Popova, n.d.).

Finding Meaning

Frankl believed that there was meaning to be had in life (Devoe, 2012). He rejected pan-determinism, a popular psychological concept that thought people had no free will and would only act on mechanical instinct. The extreme suffering observed by Frankl in the concentration camps of Auschwitz was how he first developed his ideas on how to find the meaning of life. Frankl said that suffering could be turned into achievement and accomplishment (Cuncic, 2021). For those who have gone through intense suffering, finding meaning through their suffering is said to "transform a personal tragedy into a triumph, to turn one's predicament into human achievement" (Frankl, 1992, p. 135). He witnessed prisoners with strong moral resolve who still perished in the concentration camps. This caused him to conclude that when they suffered bravely, their life had meaning even in their last moments. Therefore, he reasoned that life's meaning is not contingent on survival as a living for the sake of surviving is not a worthwhile life to love. Giving purpose to life was instilled through acts of resistance against their jailors like stealing food and singing songs (Piccirillo, 2010). Regardless of survival, they retained their identity and gave purpose to life.
Suffering is one way to find meaning through experiential values. The beauty of art and love through relationships are other ways to experience the meaningful values of life (Frankl, 1992, p. 118). Relationships

help us to understand other human beings and their potential through platonic or romantic love (Piccirillo, 2010). Experiential values require an experience such as climbing a scenic mountain and finding beauty in nature ("Pursuit of Happiness," 2021).

Aside from experiential values, there are attitudinal values and creative values. To find meaning through attitudinal values, one must change their outlook on life ("Pursuit of Happiness," 2021). Frankl used this on a patient who was depressed after the death of his wife. Frankl asked the patient if he would rather be the one who died, leaving his wife to suffer his death instead. The patient indicated that this was the worst option; in that way, the patient saw that he spared his wife from suffering.

The last way meaning can be found through values is through creative values. It requires "the widening and broadening the visual field of the patient" through creating, achieving, and accomplishing values. Engaging in pleasurable tasks like writing a novel or cultivating a garden are some ways to do so.

Techniques Employed by Logotherapy

There are three main techniques used in logotherapy: dereflection, paradoxical intention, and Socratic dialogue (Cuncic, 2021). Dereflection allows one to become whole by focusing away from the self; instead, focusing on other people. This technique is used to combat hyper-reflection, a type of anxiety when one fixates on an anxiety-provoking situation. This behaviour is commonly found in people with anticipatory anxiety. The other neurotic path dereflection can ease is hyper-intention, where one cannot achieve the goal they intend (Devoe, 2012). Frankl said that if one's goal is to achieve success, hyper-intention renders you incapable of achieving it if you overly wish for that outcome. In a study on patients with schizophrenia, it was found that these participants were more susceptible to stress (Lantz, 1982). Hyper-fixation and hyper-intention resulted from their emotional reaction to stressors. This was treated by the physician teaching the patient's family about schizophrenia and integrating their family into the treatment plan, so the family could find interests and hobbies with the patient that redirected the attention away from the diagnosis.

Next, paradoxical intention is typically used to treat anxiety or phobias by asking the patient to imagine or carry out the thing that they fear ("Pursuit of Happiness," 2021). Frankl treated a patient with hydrophobia; whenever he began perspiring, his anxiety was triggered. The patient was instructed to sweat as much as he could when his anxiety was triggered. As the patient confronts his fear, the cycle of anticipatory anxiety is broken (Cohit, 2018). The participants also become desensitized to the stimuli. Thus, the patient was successfully treated for his phobia ("Pursuit of Happiness," 2021).CBT employs a similar method to treat phobia as logotherapy does (Cohut, 2018). Some other techniques of logotherapy also coincide with cognitive behavioural therapy (CBT) or acceptance and commitment therapy (ACT), lending credence to treatment through logotherapy (Cuncic, 2021).

The final technique is Socratic dialogue, where a patient speaks to their therapist who takes note of the words and patterns in speech (Cuncic, 2021). The therapist will point out the meaning behind the words chosen, so the patient can "realize [their] own answers." Burnout from strenuous hours at work can be treated this way by a therapist asking their patient pertinent questions and self-reflecting on their frame of mind. For workers experiencing job burnout, Riethof and Bob (2019) identify the lack of meaning in work as the problem. In our capitalist society, it is becoming increasingly common for adults to have a full day of work every week instead of religious or community life (Riethof & Bob, 2019). People have external motivation for working, like being paid, which is considered a superficial goal as opposed to work that brings about purpose, fulfilment, or love for the task (Riethof & Bob, 2019; Peterson, 2021). The loss of meaningful activities in work is detrimental to mental health; thus, burnout occurs. Often, the patient's attitude can be changed, as Frankl intended, finding meaning through attitudinal values.

What is it used for?

Logotherapy helps people uncover meaning in life to reduce their feelings of "existential angst" onset by these diagnoses (Cuncic, 2010). Logotherapy is used to treat cases of compulsive disorders, obsessions, phobias, and acute stress disorder (Peterson, 2021; Madeson, 2021). Logotherapy has been found to help manage symptoms of many different maladies including anxiety, grief, guilt, pain, Post Traumatic Stress Disorder (PTSD), schizophrenia, and suicide ideation (Cuncic, 2021). Having a defined sense of meaning in life helps people to cope with their diagnoses (Peterson, 2021). In a study measuring the psychological distress in infertile women, symptoms of worry and stress were decreased after the application of logotherapy (Moslanejad & Koolee, 2013). It is also used to help patients cope with chronic illness, loss, family and relationship struggles, ADHD, Tourette Syndrome and other neurodevelopmental disorders, and addiction (Peterson, 2021). Logotherapy improved the quality of life for those diagnosed with cancer (Thir & Batthyany, 2016). Patients who suffered from cervical cancer had symptoms of depression and stress. After logotherapy, there was a significant decrease in cortisol (the stress hormone) after 6 weeks of therapeutic treatment (Soetrisno & Moewardi, 2017). In a comparable study, for patients with breast cancer, there was a significant increase in life expectancy and quality between those who underwent logotherapy treatments and the control group (Nader et al., 2019). This was attributed to the resilience developed by the patients after finding meaning in life (Madeson, 2021).

In a study at the Iranian University, logotherapy was found to reduce depression, anxiety, and PTSD in undergraduate students (Robatmili et al., 2014). More than one-fifth of the students stated that life held no meaning prior to logotherapy sessions. Participants were asked to identify meaningful values and goals for the future. This helped them to find meaning in life, reducing their depression. Robatmili et al. (2014) state that logotherapy was beneficial to these students because they have not developed a clear sense of identity due to their youth.

Logotherapy has also been applied to the mental health of immigrants who moved to Spain. Using the three techniques, the participants were allowed to be active in their own treatment (Rahgozar & Gimenez-Llort, 2020). This was found to help reduce depression and anxiety in these immigrants. For migrants who fled from war zones or persecution, logotherapy helped reduce symptoms of PTSD. In a similar study, combat soldiers afflicted with PTSD went through exercises that gave meaning to their life, leading to a decrease in stress, anxiety, and depression (Schiraldi, 2000).

Group sessions, like Alcohol Anonymous, use a form of logotherapy to rehabilitate their members (Peterson, 2021). Other addiction support groups, like ones involving narcotics, use these logotherapy techniques as well. Madeson (2021) argues that when patients see that they have freedom of will, responsibility, and life purpose they have less of a desire for mind-altering substances. Aside from addiction counselling groups, logotherapy has been observed as effective in a group of mothers of children with intellectual disabilities. Feelings of autonomy, psychological well-being, and personal growth were increased compared to a 1:1 setting between a therapist and a single patient.

Logotherapy does not always have an equally beneficial application. In regards to kidney dialysis, logotherapy improved the daily activities of patients undergoing dialysis treatment (Schwaiger et al., 2007). There are two types of dialysis either hemodialysis (HD) or continuous ambulatory peritoneal dialysis (CAPD), both of which are quite demanding. The difference is that CAPD can be done at home while HD is done under medical supervision at a dialysis centre. Overall, CAPD patients had better outcomes after logotherapy, experiencing more self-transcendence and ability to self-distance themselves, viewing themselves as not imprisoned by their personal viewpoint. The researchers propose that CAPD may be a more attractive option between the two, given that these patients were better equipped with accepting their illness than those on HD.

Scientific Validity

Due to the extreme nature of the Holocaust, there are not a lot of other events that are comparable. As such, theories and research spawned from are hard to apply to other traumatic events (Piccirillo, 2010). Elie Wiesel, another Holocaust survivor and Nobel Peace Prize laureate, wrote on the suffering he experienced in Auschwitz. He dismissed theories like Frankl's on these grounds. However, other scholars have pointed out that Dr. Frankl's account is a firsthand study of how this theory works, whereas most psychological theories rely on second or third-hand testimony.

Additionally, logotherapy is criticized as being too spiritual or religious in nature rather than a viable scientific treatment as its goal is to "heal the soul" (Peterson, 2021; Popova, n.d.). While not inherently religious, it does employ spiritual resources to withstand adversity leading some therapists to be skeptical of it (Cuncic, 2021). Not all therapists are trained in logotherapy and more research needs to be done on the exact mechanism that allows logotherapy to be therapeutic.

Furthermore, various disorders and conditions cannot be treated by logotherapy only (Gerz, 2006). In a study of phobias, 90% of the experimental group was cured or made considerable improvements using the paradoxical intention technique of logotherapy. For these patients, researchers noted that drugs and other types of therapy used in conjunction with paradoxical intention resulted in better outcomes than logotherapy alone (Gerz, 2006; Peterson, 2021).

Conclusion

Frankl believed humans have the ability to determine their existence. One can find meaning in life through suffering, relationships, and other unique experiences that add to your understanding of values. Logotherapy was developed as a mechanism to help survivors of the Holocaust heal from their trauma using dereflection, paradoxical intention, and Socratic dialogue methods. It is still used today to help treat or help ease the mind of patients who suffer through many different diagnoses.

References

Chapter 1

Melvin A. Kimble PhD & James W. Ellor PhD (2001) Logotherapy: An Overview, Journal of Religious Gerontology, 11:3-4, 9-24, DOI: 10.1300/J078v11n03_03

Piccirillo, R. A. (2010). Logotherapy and the Holocaust: Uniting Human Experience in Extremity and Normality. Inquiries Journal, 2(09).

United States Holocaust Memorial Museum. (2021, March 2). Introduction to the Holocaust: What was the Holocaust?

Viktor Frankl Institute. (1992). VFI – Viktor Frankl—Biography.

Chapter 2

Cuncic, A. (2021, July 8). What is Logotherapy? Retrieved from https://www.verywellmind.com/an-overview-of-victor-frankl-s-logotherapy-4159308#:~text=Logotherapy is a therapeutic approach,through a search for purpose.

Logotherapy. (2015, February 07). Retrieved from https://www.goodtherapy.org/learn-about-therapy/types/logotherapy#:~:text=Dereflectio : Dereflection is used when,about others rather than themselves.

Piccirillo, R. A. (2010, September 01). Logotherapy and the Holocaust: Uniting Human Experience in Extremity and Normality. Retrieved from http://www.inquiriesjournal.com/articles/289/logotherapy-and-the-holocaust-uniting-human-experience-in-extremity-and-normality

Rahgozar, S., & Giménez-Llort, L. (2020). Foundations and Applications of Logotherapy to Improve Mental Health of Immigrant Populations in the Third Millennium. Frontiers in

Psychiatry, 11, 451–451. https://doi.org/10.3389/fpsyt.2020.00451

Riethof, N., & Bob, P. (2019). Burnout Syndrome and Logotherapy: Logotherapy as Useful Conceptual Framework for Explanation and Prevention of Burnout. Frontiers in Psychiatry, 10, 382–382. https://doi.org/10.3389/fpsyt.2019.00382

Robatmili, S., Sohrabi, F., Shahrak, M. A., Talepasand, S., Nokani, M., & Hasani, M. (2015). The Effect of Group Logotherapy on Meaning in Life and Depression Levels of Iranian Students. International Journal for the Advancement of Counselling, 37(1), 54–62. https://doi.org/10.1007/s10447-014-9225-0

Viktor E. Frankl Quotes (Author of Man's Search for Meaning). (n.d.). Retrieved from https://www.goodreads.com/author/quotes/2782.Viktor_E_Frankl

Viktor Frankl. (2011, November 11). Retrieved from https://www.goodtherapy.org/famous-psychologists/viktor-frankl.html

Viktor, F. (1946). Man's Search for Meaning. Beacon Press.

Wong, P. (2017, January 02). From Viktor Frankl's Logotherapy to the Four Defining Characteristics of Self-Transcendence. Retrieved from http://www.drpaulwong.com/four-defining-characteristics-self-transcendence/

Chapter 3

Piccirillo, Ryan A. "Logotherapy and the Holocaust: Uniting Human Experience in Extremity and Normality." Inquiries Journal, Inquiries Journal, 1 Sept. 2010, www.inquiriesjournal.com/articles/289/logotherapy-and-the-holocaust-uniting-human-experience-in-extremity-and-normality.

Team, GoodTherapy Editor. "Viktor Frankl (1905-1997)." Viktor Frankl Biography, GoodTherapy, 11 Nov. 2011, www.goodtherapy.org/famous-psychologists/viktor-frankl.html.

Team, GoodTherapy Editor. "Existential Psychotherapy." GoodTherapy, GoodTherapy, 2019, www.goodtherapy.org/learn-about-therapy/types/existential-psychotherapy.

Chapter 4

Cohut, M. (2018). Logotherapy: The benefits of finding meaning in life. Medical News Today. https://www.medicalnewstoday.com/articles/320814#Current-clinical-applications-of-logotherapy.

Cuncic, A. (2021). What to Know About Logotherapy. Verywell Mind. https://www.verywellmind.com/an-overview-of-victor-frankl-s-logotherapy-4159308.

Devoe, D. (2012, July 1). Viktor Frankl's Logotherapy: The Search For Purpose and Meaning. Inquiries Journal. http://www.inquiriesjournal.com/articles/660/2/viktor-frankls-logotherapy-the-search-for-purpose-and-meaning.

Faramarzi, S., & Bavali, F. (2016). The effectiveness of group logotherapy to improve psychological well-being of mothers with intellectually disabled children. International Journal of Developmental Disabilities, 63(1), 45–51. https://doi.org/10.1080/20473869.2016.1144298

Frankl, Victor (1992). Man's Search for Meaning. (4th ed.). Boston, MA: Beacon Press.

Gerz, H. O. (2006). Experience with the Logotherapeutic Technique of Paradoxical Intention in the Treatment of Phobic and Obsessive-Compulsive Patients. American Journal of Psychiatry, 123(5), 548–553. https://doi.org/10.1176/ajp.123.5.548

Lantz, J. E. (1982). Dereflection in family therapy with schizophrenic clients. International Forum for Logotherapy, 5(2), 119–122.

Madeson, M. (2021, May 25). Logotherapy: Viktor Frankl's Theory of Meaning. PositivePsychology.com. https://positivepsychology.com/viktor-frankl-logotherapy/.

Mosalanejad, L., & Khodabakshi Koolee, A. (2013). Looking at infertility treatment through the lens of the meaning of life: the effect of group logotherapy on psychological distress in infertile women. International journal of fertility & sterility, 6(4), 224–231.Rahgozar, S., & Giménez-

Llort, L. (2020). Foundations and Applications of Logotherapy to Improve Mental Health of

Immigrant Populations in the Third Millennium. Frontiers in Psychiatry, 11, 451. https://doi.org/10.3389/fpsyt.2020.00451

Nader, M., Ghanbari, N., Tajabadi pour, S., Gholipour, S., & Esmaeilzadeh, N. (2019). Effectiveness of Short-term Group Logo-therapy on Life Expectancy and Resilience of Women With Breast Cancer. Archives of Breast Cancer, 168–173. https://doi.org/10.32768/abc.201964168-173

Peterson, T. J. (2021). Logotherapy: How It Works, Cost, & What to Expect. Choosing Therapy. https://www.choosingtherapy.com/logotherapy/.

Piccirillo, R. A. (2010, September 1). Logotherapy and the Holocaust: Uniting Human Experience in Extremity and Normality. Inquiries Journal. http://www.inquiriesjournal.com/articles/289/2/logotherapy-and-the-holocaust-uniting-human-experience-in-extremity-and-normality.

Popova, M. (2017, February 5). Viktor Frankl on the Human Search for Meaning. Brain Pickings. https://www.brainpickings.org/2013/03/26/viktor-frankl-mans-search-for-meaning/.

"Pursuit of Happiness" Viktor Frankl: Happiness and Meaning. Pursuit of Happiness. (n.d.). https://www.pursuit-of-happiness.org/history-of-happiness/viktor-frankl/.

Riethof, N., & Bob, P. (2019). Burnout Syndrome and Logotherapy: Logotherapy as Useful Conceptual Framework for Explanation and Prevention of Burnout. Frontiers in Psychiatry, 10, 382. https://doi.org/10.3389/fpsyt.2019.00382

Robatmili, S., Sohrabi, F., Shahrak, M. A., Talepasand, S., Nokani, M., & Hasani, M. (2014).

The Effect of Group Logotherapy on Meaning in Life and Depression Levels of Iranian Students. International Journal for the Advancement of Counselling, 37(1), 54–62. https://doi.org/10.1007/s10447-014-9225-0

Schiraldi, G. R. (2000). Post traumatic stress disorder sourcebook: A guide to healing, recovery and growth. Lowell House.

Schulenberg, S. E., Hutzell, R. R., Nassif, C., & Rogina, J. M. (2008). Logotherapy for clinical practice. Psychotherapy: Theory, Research, Practice, Training, 45(4), 447–463. https://doi.org/10.1037/a0014331

Schwaiger, J. P., Kopriva-Altfahrt, G., Söllner, W., & König, P. (2007). Personal abilities in patients undergoing peritoneal dialysis and hemodialysis. A pilot study using the existence scale. Wiener Klinische Wochenschrift, 119(11-12), 350–354. https://doi.org/10.1007/s00508-007-0791-6

Spear, J. (n.d.). Existential Psychology - History of the movement. History of the movement - Famous Psychologists, Existentialism, and World - JRank Articles. https://psychology.jrank.org/pages/229/Existential-Psychology.html.

Soetrisno, S., & Moewardi. (2017). The effect of logotherapy on the expressions of cortisol, HSP70, Beck Depression Inventory (BDI), and pain scales in advanced cervical cancer patients. Health Care for Women International, 38(2), 91–99.

Thir, M., & Batthyány, A. (2016). The State of Empirical Research on Logotherapy and Existential Analysis. Logotherapy and Existential Analysis: Proceedings of the Viktor Frankl Institute Vienna, 53–74. https://doi.org/10.1007/978-3-319-29424-7_7

www.ingramcontent.com/pod-product-compliance
Lightning Source LLC
Chambersburg PA
CBHW022110160426
43198CB00008B/429